UNTIL ANOTHER DAY
FOR BUTTERFLIES

First Printing 1973

Second Printing 1974

Copyright © 1973 by
Parliament Publishers
Salt Lake City, Utah
Library of Congress Catalog Card Number: 73-78102

For Mother

Who works on the weather

Acknowledgements

For their kind help and support in my finishing this book while in bed with back surgery, I would like to thank Clarice Short, Henry Taylor, Ann Stanford, Jeri Parker, and my family—Mel, Becky, Rinda, Shelley, Dinny and Megan, who are always there, with love.

Art Direction by Sherm Martin

Contents

The Beautiful Complexity

The horse under the squeaky
smelly leather
pounds between my legs
lunging past his bit
flipping clods a mile high.
My yellow floppy hat
makes creases on the wind.
Bullets of rain
beat us to the barn.

I swing down and
drop against the slick neck,
happy.
And only half the day
is gone.

Skunk Power

When the rain that's tried since noon
drops tang in the wind some skunk
must be hard put to send himself abroad.
but he manages. Out there
in some thicket of oak
his tail testing the breeze
alert or angry or struck by spring,
he ranges on the turbulence
like Gothic myths rifling
through the house opened up to June.

Cantaloupe in January

I smelled a cantaloupe just now.
I'm sure I did. I must have.
It tasted sweet and slick and bounced the boat
across the snowy yard
and we were steeping in the sun.

I was stacking haphazard sandwiches
on the leaping motormount
and spray kept needling me;
my hair flew anywhere, my bare feet steamed.

You drove in jaunty curlicues
and one of them cut the lake
sectioning the wake's meringue with a deep
ski a rope away
while all the others spilled their careful tans
on the drenched deck.

The boat marooned us in its roar
and we leaned on its instability
laughing because there was a summer
once.

Boy in the Rain

Thunder rivets me to waiting
for stuttered light
that must have been
as July sloshes off
its sweat in gutters turned
to rapids
by the rain.
I round the corner
tires plowing troughs
and see him running
barefoot
maybe nine
skinny ankle-deep
palms out and up
head back
a soggy sweater looping
inches from his naked
shiny waist.
And my bare foot
inside my shoe
is ready.

The Snowbird

Item: Jim Jacobs, known as the Snowbird, will
fly from the ridge at 2:30 p.m. and land seven
minutes later in the parking lot 2,000 feet below.

Jim Jacobs, they spread your plastic
wings strung to steel thirty feet across
to flap on snow packed by our boots
and skis in spewing from the tram.
We hundreds give you space, obsequious
as crowds around a green. And you,

sufficient, mount your skis, stomp
and grab the ropes that pull the swing-seat
tight against your hard thighs. Slim
sure Icarus, no one can, you know, fly.
Your brother even sank a year ago
on some sly void and plummeted

into pines to die trying what you try.
We all ski and call it flight, or better,
climb here into you, ready but embarrassed
at the fit. We edge the cliff that's perpendicular
and stomach-grabbing as a scaffolding
twelve stories high and make sure

your only path splits us in two.
Come on then, try it. Or give it up.
But now. Now. There. Yes. You lunge
on left ski, right, and almost left
again, then slope head first across
the cliff, drop, dangle, hang, huge wings

still to stop our frozen breath, then
Fly! You angle up some private
draft, wings working wand slow
to swoop out flat above the face
and pat the air to rise beyond
the gouged ravine: and I go

with you, able, easy, banking,
coasting, dipping, smooth as eagles
out of nests above the cabin
I used to close my eyes to ride.
You arch red and blue on purple
sky, the Snowbird no one would

believe! You even sink
to insolently slide into
the run two ridges down where I
once skied, and sear it till it ruptures
in a curve and whips you up on
breathless air across the nods of

pines, above the skeptic skiers
who cannot know: till you're blotted
on the icy sun, hybrid, distant,
miles below the parking lot,
too cold for fiery ends and aims
that never will be real again.

Until Another Day for Butterflies

Rain

Not since July
this fine fierce
aluminum

this rattle rain
this wet cocoon

to caterpillar in.

2

Too Early Spring

Mellow as the Sunday roast on Sunday air,
we left and hiked the hill, its straw mulch
like birdnest over ferns
February gray.
High up, on a lumpy crag
we backed each other's perch
and looked,
you south, me north,
you to the shrouded valley,
me to the mountains, elephant against the blue.
Back to back
we fused the day,
felt spring
at our nibbling fingers.

Capitulation

All right, all right!
Take over, Years.
Sand my layers thin.
Dry up the lubrication of becoming.
Make my bones fall thick upon each other
and disintegrate in empty hours;
turn insertions into pumice
where nerves once plumbed
the red ambrosia of too much to choose.

All right, all right!
Move in, Ruin.
Relish every thud of dropped will,
each tremor that admits the slouching beast,
the uninvited substitute for feeling leather grips,
for touching unborns
for racing suns
for sweating celebration
for tipping maybe's into yellow fields.

All right, all right—
Tonight.

Triumph

Nothing is more self-possessed than pain.
More certain of a place.
More aware of making everything aware.
It's dogged in its occupation,
Thorough in its coup.
Ambition, interest, civility and pride,
desire, curiosity,
hope,
and finally love
Give silent, sullen ground.
And pain parades
In a hollow hall.

Shot

Now, Morphine, now. Blend
   with the sheets.
Flatten feeling like
   a hose on dust.
Spread me liquid along
   the shudder where
my legs have been. Melt
   my hips. Flood
the ragged heaviness
   along my back.
Fizz it out my
   airy palms. Now
my head. Swamp
   the squirming. Let
it drown. Then if
   it dries, curl it
up to roll away
   and corner sleep.

No. Don't slither
   off in trails of
me. Don't wisp away
   like fumes at inter-
sections. Don't lump
   me here on this
fierce bed to wait.

Set Back

The cave gets deeper, swallowing itself
and me, its walls other days.
It crushes me against its sallow sides,
my pupils huge with hunger for the light
shining yellow on openings
lost beyond the labyrinths.
The cave closes
and tightens
in another spasm
as I am thrust toward black
and cold
and ends.

Abide

Last night I tried to remember
laughing
but my cheeks hung like
bagged sand
and my eyeballs burned behind
themselves.

My drought pinched out only
whimpers
for You to hear.
But now, today,
my hollows fill.
Again You
managed rain.

Yes!

Hey World! Good morning.
Today I'm cured for sure.
Watch me swing out of bed
and take my tongs to everything
not where it should be! Dirty clothes,
you're sunk. Weeds, hang on to your roots.
Hunger, you'll be fed—by me, myself.
Personally I'll stir juice and beat with a wooden spoon
and indulge any fancy that
makes it up the stairs.

Take me off. Spirit me away
through petunias and geraniums
and the birch that never really learned
how to cry. I'll catch whatever
you can throw and pin it high
on the gray grapestake that
fences not a thing.

3

Ninety-five

Welcome to my attic.
It's small and crowded
But where I spend me.
No one comes
At least not now.
Why should they?
No one knows my name.
Oh, certainly, that—
Aunt Kate, Miss Stayner.
But not my name.

No one knows a thing.
Who ever saw me dance
    or ride the pinto at the Fair
    or snitch Brother Brewer's cherries
    or catch the street car
    or drive an auto before the mayor could
    or buy a radio that got New York
    or sell twenty-seven ads one month
    or hear Myrt and Marge at 9 five nights a week
    or be a missionary in Detroit
    or sing for Rueben—high C—even him surprised
    or make a flowered hat
    or get some land to give away
    or see Alaska
    or watch his buggy disappear behind the dust?
See my boxes full of boxes.
Open them enough
And here I am:
Too far away for anyone
To call me Katherine.

Friend

Neither knows
who called
or why,
only that
we're here.

Megan and Bently

The little dog would follow her, of course,
the ten-year-old with hair spread-eagling
from two elastics, with violin and hoppy-taw
and school to go to. Escaped, he minces
jagged arrows through her short cuts
and barks proprietarily at cars
or distant dogs or clumps of dirt,
airily suspicious of her friends,
head never higher than when she pats it,
leaves and disappears beyond the doors
beyond the steps he's learned to stay below
and wait
until she runs again
to show him where his pleasure lies.
But more, much more, she'll need
than even what those doors reveal;
and hers will be a thousand courses
no mincing, proprietary step can find.

English 183: 3 Hours Credit
Goodbye Jon Kerowski
Go Well Doralee Dodd

Goodbye Jon with Jesus eyes and scorn for imitation
who couldn't make the crush into Spenserian Stanzas

Jon whose wire-rims and pony-tail scooped protest out of
Wordsworth daffodils, sure that Le Roi Jones fisted back

Jon surprised to look at mountains, who wouldn't say it all
because the sophomore girls saw unbruised metaphors

Jon Kerowski gently writing "pig" in lower case: May
the dragon draft sweep somehow past your crossed door.

And Doralee, Miss Idaho, blonde oppressor
of a head discharged to match that face and body

Doralee whose fragments spill on Yeats and Bethlehem,
to skitter for the A I ache to give to ballet:

Go well, Doralee Dodd stumbling in impossibles, too young
to recognize the roots that grow out brown; dance light

And may the choreography that spouts your *tour jetés*
smooth salve upon the cold destruction of wanting more.

First Loss

My grandma shared her bed with me,
Till she died when I was twelve.
We slept with breaths that matched.
(I went to sleep every night restraining
Deliberately one extra breath in five
To let her slower time teach mine to wait.)

She never knew I waited, but talked
To me of Mendon where Indians ferreted
Her isolated young-wife home for cheese and honey,
And of Santa Barbara and eerie tides that
Drew her now for gentle months away from snow,
And sometimes of Evangeline lost in the forest primeval.

Grandma's batter-beating, white-gloved, laughing
Daytime self slept somewhere else, and she visited
Melifluous beyond my ardent reach, always off
Before me. I followed into rhythms I knew
Were good, her chamois softness weighing me
By morning toward a cozy common center.

She died there, when I was twelve.
I was sleeping, alien, down the hall
In a harder bed, isolated from the delicate
Destruction that took its year to take her.
That night my mother barely touched my hair
And in stiff, safe mechanics twirled the customary

Corners of my pillow one by one. "Grandma's gone,"
She said. Crepuscular against the only light
Alive behind her in the hall, she somehow left.
My covers fell like lonely lead on only me.
I lay as if in children's banks of white where
After new snow we plopped to stretch and carve

Our shapes like paper dolls along a fold.
Now, lying on my back, I ran my longest arms
From hip to head, slow arcs on icy sheets,
And whispered childhood's chant to the breathless room:
"Angel, Angel, snowy Angel,
"Spread your wings and fly."

Mosaic

the gray mosaic day
collects itself
clutching
corners
spreading aimlessly
across
the hours

untouched
stick figures flop
into
spaces
labeled occupied
and do
their ordered
calesthentics

edgeless
every day
goes hunting
you

Faces Under the Dryer at Robert Steur's College of Beauty

Faces on the heads
pinned and tinned
baking
mesmerized by silence
only noice can make.

Isolated
in torpedoed uniformity
insulated
in a twenty-minute blow
from lying
dyeing
trying.

Unposed
waxen real
any minute they'll explode
into some unsuspecting orbit
leaderless
and
not about to care.

Lucy
Mummy: Pueblo, Female, Age 33

Lucy—you'll go with me, Lucy, when I leave,
Your wretched smile all that's left to see.
The rest of you is charred forgettables
Glassed over, blacked out, stashed away like
Your empty husk. In your sandstone cliff,
Ledged below the hundred footholds, you ate
Your demon corn turned into bread in rock
Metates that sifted grit into your
Stunted life and ground your teeth to here.
Now they'll shred my nights with wondering how
You finally died. What pain so smashed itself
Across your mouth? Fright never stayed like that,
Nor even agony. What got you, grimaced
Ghost that you can leave your sawed-off teeth in me?

Repair

The lights were out
all over
and the man who came

ran his green truck
into our
driveway because of

the pole. My T
V and stove,
washer, iron and

lights were out and
I'd flipped all
the switches in the

box from on to
off and back
and nothing had hap-

pened. So when this
man arrived
with his starched name on

his green shirt I
was glad. In
fact when he climbed the

pole step by step
and dangled
there and fiddled with

things and the lights
came on I
said now there's a man!

Confirmation

(For Clarice Short, teacher of poetry)

In your cathedral classroom, students stared
and shivered as your skeptic eye prepared
a coffin for their muted, worried words.

Rooted in your pulpit, you invoked
a windowed sky for tokens, looking
for that quick camaraderie of knowing.

But how to lubricate austerity?
How to hide the stifling, stern despair
of never quite expecting what you heard?

Certainties bequeathed their loneliness to you,
triggering the ball-points that recorded new
the ancient quiet company of your

proud chamber. But now, these thinking months away
from my contentions with your enigmatic gaze
at skies not mine to see, I capitulate:

My little mind strings certainties across
the chasms where I sometimes leap because
of catechisms learned in pressured awe.

Mother

She's dying, like Job beyond the circumstance,
as the heart too big pumps less and less
in classic calm.
Concerned with living and the live
she plans for Christmas
intent on what has been,
in reluctant rummaging of what will be.
The grip is tight as solder,
blue-flamed in years of fired belonging
first to them, now to us.
And she cannot let go
any more that we can undo our fingers
clinging to the right to cling.

Climbing into the Sea
(To Lyle—Killed in an old war)

In the heat of the summer he climbed
Up the far, pine side of the knoll,
Padding the needle-soft path.
But through the desperate shadows of endings,
The camera he clutched was useless
For the light, elusive and rising,

Rose with the sunset and doffed our chance
For one last clutch at the summit and sun.
As he arrowed up deer trails, he checked
Me straggling behind, and tendered the branches
That threatened me and his thrust to the ridge,
And his black hair was curled with the climb.

Then he stood on the darkened rise with triangled arms,
Chest arching, nose spread with the sage and
Mahogany, swallowing sorrow with the squirrel
Who squabbled alone in the pine. Coming down
He was silent except for his shoes, his run jolting smooth
What he had to run. Next day he flew off

To a carrier base and a catapult fused
To a twisting deck that would fling him a mile
At the sun, guns blazing their incantations, him
Strewn in strange joy on the orange, the finally orange
Sky. When they said how he'd died within sight
Of the convoy, gas in both engines gone,

I could see him scorning the obvious plunge,
Coasting instead on the switch-backs, carving a path
To the sea. He'd calculate up-drafts and ride them,
Volcanoes of moments to palm him gently down
To the void of choiceless deciding, his ships
Now sightless, their movement decreed, churning

And lugging the ill fitting shroud of departure.
Years later I look at a down-going fire
And see him, his plane flopped flat on the water,
Rise from the cockpit, and climbing
From watery wing to wave, still goggled, intact,
His flight boots, giant, filling and sucking him

Under, his cap tight snapped, clinging to green
As a parachute would to blue, locking his jaw
In a smile as he settles everything—into the sun.

The Hut

They haul the blistered boards
from anywhere
lurching up the undergrowth
to where their secret place
will rise.

Shaky shovels flatten out
a rooted, earthy floor
and knotty 2 x 4's and
peeling plywood wobble
on unsteady nails packed
crooked into constellations
of half-moon misses.

For six days the canyon
has echoed their building,
bouncing off
uncertain saws and
treacherous hammers.

Today they called it done
and went to playing mumble peg.
They pass it coming and going
to the swing, but
what do you do with
a finished secret hut?

4

I Marry You

What was I?
What roused my day?
What pampered night?
What brought yellow roses hovering about
 like fairies that scampered
 from my childhood
 when the light went on
 but left their whimsey
 for my private eyes?
What is it that you bring?

What was I? What gave the salt,
 the burning clove?
 What rescued quietly abandoned dreams
 like plankton moving
 toward the unseen motion
 of a changing moon?
Where have you taken me?

Before the bringing
 and the taking,
what made me know enough
 to marry you?

the keys are lost

the keys are lost. where can they be found?
in silent places with their jumbled parts
they loosely turn and turn and turn around.

nostalgia twists the need they plumb to sound
tight openings with vacancies for hearts.
the keys are lost and where can they be found?

is it the keys that keep the Keeper bound?
or where they used to fit? what missing starts
the awful turn and turn and turn around?

did thieves thrust early into threads that wound
unwatched and well through years of easy starts?
before the keys were lost, jangling to be found?

through rings and rings of keys the search is bound
to finger holes that substitute for hearts:
they all will turn and turn and turn around.

what combination thrashes for its count?
who knows the will of keys and holes and parts?
the keys are lost and even if they're found,
won't they still just turn and turn and turn around?

Things That Don't Change
Change the Most

The car ferrets up the one-way
tunneled green
by instinctive turns
at last across the
lumpy bridge (that
8 x 8 was high and
heavy even for my
brothers) and onto
needled grass.

I park below the pines
with my changes
and huddle up the will
to walk the creek bed path
alone
to changeless things.

First roll the window.
Hear the streams converge,
their pungent woody banks
delivering us as children
wet like puppies
stomping in the dust
to cake our guilty boots
in camouflage,
our darkest sin
a wade or fall to clutch
the clumpy moss that peeled
like avocado from
only center rocks.

Plush green
the moss is there again
still.
I squeeze the handle
push the door
move along the stream,
the path the same
aspen birch and dogwood held:
there the cabin
brown ripple stained
from sodden snow
as rustic as
belief in changelessness
and now as real.

I go slow and soft
breathing up the tasteless courage
to remind my flaking years
The changeless changes most.
So let the cabin in.

Ending

I feel your going drag at me behind
a craggy hand gnarled by nearness, thickened
by the callouses of crises. I'm sickened
by its sure, abrasive pull and hold back, blind
to imminence, a child still dawdling
over getting dressed to leave. I touch and
try to gather you and me—wispy strands
to fortify ascetic days, maudlin
scraps of tender time—a note, a candle
fingered full of just-right hollows, wrinkled
rooms of loosened strings.
                              But no. I think I'll
leave them clearly labeled Do Not Handle
and let this going pull me stripped and stark
beyond the clutching, new and clean and dark.

Unmatched Pair

The lathered withers of
the chestnut mare still
ripple involuntarily,
her head abrupted in
bewildered eyes at being
held, lobotomized

       connected to

            a harness strained to
            string, limp down the thick
            neck of the hulk which
            if it plods at all, is
            guarded, grounded,
            striving just to put
            shoe ahead
            of shoe.

The Blue Tattoo

*(On hearing of an offer by the medical school
to pay $1,000 cash for claim on any body)*

A thousand dollars now (cash).
And who'd know but me? And maybe whoever
keeps the record or does the tattoos.
A thousand dollars now, cash.

A little blue tattoo on my right big toe
saying I'm theirs, no matter when I die.
What difference would it make when I'm dead?
Who ever thinks of bodies anyhow, in graves—or labs?

> Dr. Kiwamoto took us in Anatomy One
> past the door with black letters "Medical
> Students Only" (The Gross lab). He understood
> how boring plastic (all parts removable) models
> and pickled putty-colored embryos could get.
> (He laughed a lot.)

I wonder if they'd let me buy me back, maybe
with interest. Sometime when a thousand dollars
wouldn't mean a thing.

> The rich formaldahyde, the wrinkled sheet,
> the swoop that bared the gray green (like
> Kindergarten clay) cadaver.

How awful would the wondering become? How urgent
not to die? How careful would I be, tattooed with
brittle fear? I could fool them all. And chop
or blow my toe off. And only limp. Or have a
plastic surgeon sand the blue away.

Sliced smooth from sternum to groin
the stubbled (they say they grow hair and
fingernails after they die) man lay parted
like Grand Canyon, one side cavernous
beside the severed cliff impressed
with fossils and striations of what
used to work. And neatly along the hollow
(clean but green) a lined-up liver, lung,
spleen, intestine, and (How lucky he'd not
had it out!) appendix scalpeled smooth
for an A in Gross.

A thousand dollars now, cash.
I'm not my body, flesh, a pound of nothing,
parts assembled to be manipulated by me (in essence).

"He's Pierre." The doctor smiling, flinging
the smell across the dead (dead) man. "Some
guys get so used to this they eat their lunch
while they carve."

You can get up to five-hundred dollars just for
your eyes. And what's the price for flying
into myself intact, Sistine fingers reaching (almost),
my God?

Now Winter

Like a snowflake on the tongue
                our time is gone,
This winter fall when white
                hushed over dun
Before October. I see
                the old mountains
Humping in their cloaks, purple
                at this frigid
Passing, and long to pull
                their pink skull caps
Back for one more hour of you.
                I lift my head,
Turn my tingling inside out,
                and drive away,
Juxtaposed beside a tranquil me
                that whispers
"Take your time." I do. I will.
                It's what I have.

Afterwards

The worst is stumbling
onto last times,
your wheres and whens.
Resolve is flimsy gauze
against the razors
of remembering.

Conversion

I forget when I'm away
the throb, unsolicited as hurt
that inundates my reason.
Often exiled in doubts
inflamed by dogma's small discipleship
I pull away
sure the hand I feel in mine
leads anywhere but here.

But here again,
some quiet note can resonate
in chambers secret and persuasive
as being homesick
on a trip designed to get away.
And I come surging home
to You.

5

Reunion — Class of '41

Where are you La Dena Pack, Stewart John
    Haputman, Geraldine Midgely?
Barbara Stuki, Richard Hoyt Isenberg,
    what are you being in '71?
The letter, red, white and urgent,
    listed you missing, classmate,
you and two-hundred and seventy-three
    others whose faces smile forever
in the golden Eastonia of nineteen-hundred
    and forty-one.

You pocked the same desks, basketed the same
    balls, smelled the same Bunsen Burners;
you danced lip-to-forhead in the squeaky
    ballroom, hoarsed the same exultant vivos;
you smoked behind the tennis courts or slept
    through early seminary; you cheered the long kiss
in "My Maryland" and stashed black-edged pages
    of Hemingway in your tall locker; you sang
Lisle Bradford's hallelujahs and collected your diploma
    from our one-eyed principal.

Thirty years between you and that staunch smile,
    the committee says come home. Into
what parentheses have you vanished?
    Are your indelibles so pale? Are the cozy
Salt Lake boundaries so awash with close-ups
    that you who fade beyond the womb
immaterialize like fog in wind?

Frances De Niel Burman, Anna Rae Pearch,
    Keith Sherman Potts, I hope you
get up this morning and are found.

Spook Alley

They've lived here
most of their lives.
Some are nearly grown
and you'd expect that
they could take the hall
without a light
and find their way.

But when they shut it off
it crawls inside itself
and in the dark they scream
and feel for anything
that isn't there,
hoping desperately not
to find each other.

There's no air, and after
five minutes of curdled
closeness, it swirls with
swampy terror. They come
out with golf ball eyes,
drowning, thrashing
for a door and a place.

Iron Lung

They can't resist.
Every time we pass
They gape at the

Three-paneled window
Checking if she's
There, the lady they've

Never seen who lives
In the iron lung,
The beige and black

Barrel beyond the
Shimmering glass on
The curve at the top

Of the hill where
We turn to go to
The store. They

Used to wonder how
She ate and why
She could only

Talk in spurts. They've
Quit asking how it
Works. They just

Crane silently (I
Wonder if they
Know they do.)

They know I had a
Friend die once in
One of those. They

Know the power has
To stay on, maybe
From her basement

Generator in a
Storm, or she can't
Breathe. Now they

Only look. But
Every time. And sit
Back satisfied that

She's there. One
Day the drapes were
Drawn and no one

Spoke clear to
The store and back
When she was

There again. What
Will happen if
The lung is ever

Gone? How will we travel
Where we have to?
And how long will they

Be bound like tongues in
Search of nerves to probe
The awful vacancy?

On Hitting a Ball — Square

It must seem stupid.
Unless of course you've hit a ball—square:
And felt the thud of swift surprise slam
into your palm

and through your wrist
and up your arm,
splitting your chest
and sending your brain off quivering in waves

that giddy out and ricochet off fences
and clouds and mountains
and bounce back into your brain
and chest and arm and wrist and palm,

claiming you forever victim
of rash expectancy that what incredible phenomena
connived to let your eye and hand connect
with whatever ball you hit—square—

will somehow surely mesh again
and swat you reeling
back and back and back and back
to hit another ball.

Hall of Eyes

It started when I forgot
to turn the light on
in the hall where our
black framed family
pictures starch against
their following.

In the dark they watched,
squaring uranium teeth
on my brief solitary walk.
And I felt their pink soft
suggestions fingering for
my hand.

Since then I've been hurrying
with my plastic poncho kicking
up a breeze that no eyes can
open in. Except I think
I never really wanted
to get here all alone.

Timing

This morning a swarm of sparrows
left late from Fall,
clustered in brown sputters on the winter sky, then
dropped like splotches onto
the arthritic arms of the birch.

"Birds! Birds!" she cried, the nine-year-old,
and fled to find the crackling bread
cornered in the bin for such a day.

But when she spread her crumbs, expectant,
on the icy patio, the sparrows lifted,
undulating like a speckled veil
borne off by wind.

She stood there, puzzled at their nonsense,
waiting, certain they'd return to claim
with their stacatto heads her banquet.

But sparrows know their way,
and crumbs were late and little.

Christmas Eve

Captive on the crinkled edge of childhood,
Nudging through impatient sighs I see
Your packaged promises of morning
Whose undoing will so disenchant you, Tree.

Your predecessors willow here like fires
Each an embered year whose poignant glow
Tinsels me to Grace and rare acceptance
For this night at least, of all I need to know.

I tissue in your branches somehow hoping
Your pagan warmth can help me to be sure
That Bethlehem bequeathed for more than Christmas
This expectation that tomorrow can endure.

Sunday School Picture

1   Our Ward housed
the biggest Sunday School the Church has ever
let exist, and one Sunday morning a thousand
of us hipped into the breathless benches
and undulated into the foyer, ante room,
recreation hall, and up onto the indignant stage
a thousand Mormon heads away from the pulpit.

                    In the picture
that President Heber J. Grant had them take
that auspicious day (three shots overlapping)
I came out twice, being on the edge of two of them,
and Mother always said that would guarantee me
two chances at perfection, but I being seven
at the time figured so? and went on becoming
two people instead.

2   One me would chin
my fretted flimsiness the forty-three times
my brothers said I should be able to
on the banister in the empty entry of the Ward,
and blithely loosen the screen from inside
the classroom while my Primary teacher
was rasping at Donnie Rohlfing,

                            so my brothers
and I and certain franchised friends could
scrunch in later and titter nonsense from
the palsied pulpit and play The Happy Farmer

with our pleated fingers on the cool black pedals
of the organ, and with rapid eyes see what other
kinds of bathrooms looked like, and run tautly for our
window if Mr. Tomlinson came clinking in,
and then try not to sit by Richard when I needed
to be nice in church

                    because he was the brother
that I got the giggles with like when we sang
You-hoo unto Jesus and had to leave all the time
hunching up the searing aisle acting like
we had the nosebleed, and Richard who was five
in First Grade when I was four in Kindergarten
smiled the teacher into promoting me into
his class (no one seemed to mind as long as I
could read the flash cards)

                    so I could be
on first and catch the siren balls he practiced
on me in our shivering front room where no one ever
threw anything except when Father thought
the quickest way to get me dressed for church
was to juggle my patented leather paraphernalia
at me saying Think fast!

                    so I'd snatch them on
before they dropped to prove I could, and then
race across the mud-hard fields to beat the organ's
going silent whispering its Sunday sentence.

3   The other me sedately
bathed my Di Dee Doll till her left eye
washed away, and played house with Corinne

at least seventeen hours a week in the tolerant
trailer her father built, and hated it when Marilyn
Mason (it must have been because of her wet palms
that stuck to things) beat me once a day
all summer at jacks,

              and lady-like
read Polly Anna, certain of a tunnel (probably
under our hollyhocks) and wrote a poem
drying my tortuous ringlets by the radiator
in the bathroom about spilling batter
on the blue kitchen floor that pale Miss Crawford
announced I must have copied somewhere,

and that me sat in buttoned velvet memorizing
the swollen arch of the ward chapel that cupped
the painting of the Sacred Grove where green
bumped into blue like my 500 piece puzzle with 200
desperate pieces of sky,

              and hoped that
the deacons were noticing that I could read
the words to I Know That My Redeemer Lives,
which I wondered why we sang all four verses to
even though I was sure I guess I did know,
and recited a two-and-a-half minute ordeal
that my mother knew I knew on Why I Want
To Be Baptized,

              which I didn't because of
the hospital and Richard who was in there
and couldn't be baptized with me, and pushed
one fidget finger at a time into the tempting
screw holes in the boring bench in front,

and dangled and waved absently with the other
eight-and-unders in the choir seats at our
determinedly non-noticing mothers,

and that me
made handkerchief dolls with my eyes closed
during the prayer and searched the sacrament
for the bread without a crust and held the rim
of the kiss-size cup against my lip and swallowed
slow to let it trickle down and feel like what
they said it should, and tried to think of Jesus
all white like in the Grove, not with his beard
crumpled on his collar bone, dead.

4   Sometimes I look
at that thousand-peopled picture when I'm sorting
things and marvel a lot, and even otherwise, I find
myself saying, Highland Park Ward, my roller skates
still rattle down your dented driveway, and
my absent waiting is sometimes done against
the brown banisters below the Garden of Gethsemane
in your raised entry,

and mostly, your organ
churns under its outside loft across the filled
fields where our short-cuts are long buried
in old foundations,

and like the green-grained oak
of your chapel doors, it closes with gentle right
my separateness and gathers my wandering
double selves together.